MW00514326

Thinking with Poetry

Thinking with Poetry

Constantina C. D. Hodnett

VANTAGE PRESS
New York

Published by Vantage Press, Inc.
419 Park Ave. South, New York, New York 10016

Manufactured in the United States of America
ISBN: 978-0-533-12726-9

Library of Congress Catalog Card No.: 98-090155

0 9 8 7 6 5 4 3 2 1

To Alexander Christopher Hodnett and future generations

Contents

Acknowledgments

The people in my life who have encouraged my writing career were a high school teacher and a college professor, who was also a columnist for a local newspaper.

While not being a journalism major in college, I did receive recognition for excellence in the writing of critiques, term papers, and similar writing competitions.

I wish to thank the *World of Poetry* of Sacramento, California, for publishing my first poems, "Wishing Well," in their yearly book *Anthology of Poetry,* in 1990, along with several awards and certificates. These achievements gave me incentive to continue writing an accumulation of additional poems, into the making of a more creative thinking.

About the Author

Constantina Cecelia DeShields Hodnett was born on July 26, 1948, in Baltimore City, Maryland, to the parents, Constantina Hudgins DeShields and Houston Randolph DeShields. Having met as students at Carver Vocational High School, her mother studied Practical Nursing, and her father studied Electrical Engineering. This small family of three then later moved to the lower Eastern Shore of Maryland to live and to grow, to a family of six. The new siblings included a brother, Randolph Joseph DeShields; a sister, Jeanette Francine DeShields; and the youngest brother, Jude Thaddeus DeShields.

At ages four and five, Constantina began kindergarten at the Odd Fellows Hall summer school, for two seasons. Elementary education began at the Ross Street Elementary School in Snow Hill, Maryland, for six more years. In 1959, junior and senior high school education resumed for six more years, at the new Worcester High, in Newark, Maryland.

Before graduation at Worcester, on June 9, 1966, many awards, honors, and certificates were received in business, typing, shorthand, band, and science, in addition to four years in the National Honor Society.

By graduation, two scholarships were received, one to Strayer, a two-year junior college in Alexandria, Virginia, and another four-year scholarship to Morgan State University, in Baltimore, Maryland, which was later transferred to Salisbury State University, Salisbury, Maryland. After this, there was, at last, a graduation in the Winter Class of 1977, earning a Bachelor of Science degree in Liberal Studies, with a concentration in Elementary Education.

After graduation, a variety of teaching experiences were gained as a Substitute Teacher at the Snow Hill Middle School, the Snow Hill Elementary School, and as a Nursery School Teacher at the Jack-and-Jill Day Care Center, in Snow Hill, also. Along with teaching, further studies were resumed at the Institute of Children's Literature. From the institute in Redding Ridge, Connecticut, a diploma was received in 1983, in a Writing and Publication Course.

Along with Writing and Publishing, an additional certificate was received from Art Instruction Schools, in Basic Art, in 1985 from Minneapolis, Minnesota. Besides writing poetry, a particular liking, Constantina has enjoyed writing articles, speeches, and children's stories. An additional part-time teaching experience includes Home/Hospital Teacher at the Pocomoke High School.

On March 21, 1979, nuptial vows were exchanged between childhood sweethearts, Members of the 1965 Worcester Graduating Class. In downtown Snow Hill, Herman A. Hodnett, Jr. (III) (1947–1994) and Constantina C.D. Hodnett were married.

A year later, on January 4, 1980, to this union Alexander Christopher Hodnett was born. We enjoyed years of marriage in the town of Pocomoke. Growing up in Pocomoke City, Maryland, Alexander began his education in Stockton, Maryland at the Head Start Program. Later on, he entered into kindergarten at the Pocomoke Elementary School. Then, Pocomoke Middle School also proved to be successful with many ribbons and awards in the "Book It" incentive reading program.

As a student in Pocomoke High School, Alex played drums in the band and was a member of the editorial staff on the school newspaper. After graduation in 1998, he was accepted and entered the United States Army at Fort Jackson, South Carolina.

Alex was also a student of dance for two years at the Dance Loft, in downtown Pocomoke. His course of study included tap and ballet. At the end of the year, all categories and age groups performed in full dress, in the auditorium at Pocomoke High School.

Alexander is currently a student at Coppin State University, in Baltimore City, Maryland. He is a Computer Sciences major. He made a 4.0 during his very first semester. Besides being a veteran of the Army, he was a graduate from Fort Lee, Virginia. He later served a year in South Korea and another year in Iraq. He was in the 3rd MP Regiment, Enduring Freedom, and while there, he received many awards as well as receiving an honorable discharge with the rank of seargeant.

Introduction

Thinking with Poetry is an accumulation of creative writings. Each poem is intended to leave with the reader a sense of enlightenment and encouragement to some form of self-actualization.

Inner strength can be found in many ways. However, reading is always meant to be a learning experience. Reading should always be an activity of intellectual insight and thinking.

I hope that through each page you, the reader, will feel uplifted and realize that there are many ways to open the mind. Journey through these items of thought and be a part of my collection of insights into positive thinking.

Thinking with Poetry

Miracles

Who believes in miracles?
People who hope, people who search,
People who look for the truth,
Those who believe in miracles
Look up to the Supreme Being.
Look up towards the roof.

To believe in miracles
Means to grow in wisdom and love,
Cleansing the body and the soul.
We constantly remember our Creator,
On earth, in the sea and the heaven above.

Children believe in miracles.
They believe in love.
Caring and growing,
And knowing that God is above.

Who believes in miracles?
Only those who have learned
The real meaning of existing;
It was love that brought us here.
And it is love to make a wish,
Every creature changes and grows.
This is a part of living.

What is a miracle?
It is a simple thought,
More spiritual than physical,
And certainly nothing bought.
For a miracle is also everlasting,
Like a wish and a beautiful butterfly,
To be caught.

A miracle is more than wishful thinking,
More than a dream,
More than the food we eat,
And more than the water we're drinking.

To believe in oneself and the infinite,
A miracle is perfect, pure and complete.
For it is greater than the tangible and now,
To believe in a time ahead, the future we see,
A light-world as long as and as wide as we want it to be;
This is how great my miracle can be.

Magic

Tell me a story about magic,
And we shall surely see
How we have strayed so far
From a world of majesty and glory.

Can men really move mountains
And grow a tree out of a mustard seed?
And can a single thought blossom and grow
To materialize into fruitful wonders indeed?

Tell me a story about magic
About why bees hum, and birds fly,
And I can also tell you
That having faith in oneself is truth, and not a lie.

In this universe, there is a source of
Energy that we call God, others call Sun.
Full of warmth and glowing wonder too.
For there is a magic called *life,*
In many forms, shapes and sizes,
Even inside of us, born anew.

Tell me a story about magic,
A *constant* renewal of life,
In all of its many forms,
Flowers, trees, animals, you and me
And realize that all of this is in
God, you, and me, we are all as one, you see.

The Prince and His Power

Who is this Prince, a handsome Prince,
A fancy man and His Power?
A hunger for grandeur, a hunger for greatness,
The world, He seems to devour.

With wealth and fame, a magical claim,
To genius, to influence of this hour;
Women find him charming.
Men find him alarming;
And they're all after the same thing, power.

Princess and princesses, kings and queens,
Of royalties both great and small,
We all breathe of this air, we all
Live on this earth because God loves us all.

There is the bitter with the sweet.
There is the small with the great.
There is the good, and there is the bad.
There is the love, and there is the hate.

But should we all cease to remember
That the ultimate power comes from above,
From our teacher, our author, and our creator,
Who told us that not through war, that not through
Hate, and not from chaos do we thrive?
But to love and to share, and by showing that we care,
These are the real reasons we are all alive.

Gods and goddesses, creatures both great and small,
As little we sit, as tall we stand, God made us all.
On our planet and on others,
Are we really worlds apart, at all?

We are many Adams, we are many Eves.
We are both the givers and the takers.
There are many planets, and there are many suns,
And there are many moons, of the created, not the makers.

But there is only one Great God;
And there is only one Great Sun,
In this universe, of course, only one creation
Began with the courtship between sun, moon and earth.
Between God, man and woman.

And it's through this courtship.
And it's through this marriage, that He knows
Us so very much.
He knows our feelings, He knows our thoughts.
He created us from a simple touch. . . .

A simple touch started it.
A simple touch made it; a small touch, only
The slightest impulse can travel so far
From the center of one being,
In this universe, reaching any star.

Is there life on other planets?
Of course there is, there is valid proof
That they are aware of our presence here.
There is valid proof that they have observed the love
Between ourselves, our towns, our states and our
        countries.
There is valid proof that God is both near and far,
And not just in the heavens, in the distance above the
        trees.

God is near and far, short and tall.
He comes to us through marriages, between men and
women.
He comes to us in a feeling, in a thought.
He is the King of the Universe.
God is love, the Prince of Power, and in us all.

Blessings to the Unborn

Nature has her secrets
To nurture and to protect,
All precious forms of life,
Especially the young in danger of neglect.

The animal kingdom can be
Ever so unpredictable and ever so cruel.
To include all of the species,
Who sometimes waver from the Golden Rule.

There are a variety of forms
Of life in various sizes and shapes,
Insects, fishes, birds and bees,
All kinds of fruits, flowers and trees.

Feelings are great to continue life,
Meaning also to include those about to come.
We must always welcome the newborn,
Into the plane of the living and try not to scorn.

For we ourselves were once newcomers,
Of new life so tender and so sweet,
Someone loved and cared for us,
From a tiny first hair, down to our tiny baby feet.

Why should we pretend to be so blind
And so full of vanity fair and pride,
To deny someone else, the glory,
That is welcome to us all, acceptance from deep down
        inside.

The right to life is more than a privilege,
Much more than fun and games;
It is our responsibility to the chain of life,
God's command and our duty, all the same.

And now I am sharing this bit of news.
Who are we to criticize and scorn?
We can't afford to scoff or curse,
But must remember from where we came,
And may God bless the unborn.

Eyes of Heaven

The eyes of heaven are many;
They are all forms of life,
Created by our all-knowing One,
Both eyes of daylight and eyes of night.

Just imagine that every eye is His,
The eyes of eagles and of every bird,
The eyes of EVERY sighted being,
A visionary gift that is both camera and word.

The eyes of heaven are both precious and good,
For God loves His creations of beauty,
Every blade of grass, every flower,
To include fishes of the seas, as best that He could.

Every kind of creature, to mean exactly that,
From every wiggly, crawly, creeping thing,
Farm animals and woodsy animals,
Inclusive of a typical dog or cat.

God has a very wonderful plan,
And as always it includes woman and man,
A likable pair we all are,
Birds of the air, fishes in the sea, and the animals on land.

One man could not see with his eyes,
Because he had been blind,
But yet he could see in other ways,
By touching and listening, a different sense of sight and
     mind.

A different sense of sight and mind,
Yet all of the same visionary kind.
We have intelligent sense and common senses,
They were always there all the time.

And so, we too are members of the
Eyes of heaven to the ONE we call GOD.
He watches and guides us toward the light.
He greatly loves us and He greatly cares for us,
All day and all night.

Love Magic

There is a mystical magic, which comes from above,
A kind of magic, yet to be defined,
Between man and woman, a thing called love,
A wonderful feeling, wonderful enough to be divine.
Exactly what does happen when boy meets girl?
Is it hypnotism, a spell-binding magic?
Or could we also say that this alluring charm
Is only to be expected of us all, all around the world?
None of us can be so sure as to say,
And none of us can be positive enough;
For those of us who experience the feeling,
Because, we are said to possess, just the right stuff.

Now then, who decides which man?
And then, who decides which woman?
To compromise and hypnotize,
A union inherited from Eve and Adam.
Love is thought to be good,
And then again, it should,
For it symbolizes a union of the spirit, the mind, the body,
Giving us childhood, adolescence, and adulthood.
Why then, do some people misuse and abuse,
Something which is taught to be so sacred,
A gift of love, which comes from above,
A God-given right and privilege to use?

The seeds of knowledge have continuously grown
Since the day Eve discovered in paradise
That power of speech and promise of something better,
Depends upon what we reap, by what is sown.
The spirit ventures very far and very wide,
Testing us all of our very pride.

Needless to say what any of us would do,
To have a very special dream come true.
We have learned that experience is the best teacher,
As many of us have before learned and learned,
That knowledge is king, and a great stepping-stone,
For honors won and honors earned.

The mystical magic of love is wonderful indeed,
To the lucky few who can plant the seed,
A flower to grow and to nourish from love,
Because the Planner plants the seeds of love from above.
One country apart, a few hours away,
Resolving a scary divorce.
My husband refuses to free me,
So that I can love and marry again, another day.
If only Allah would help me,
And see my freedom more, to see,
How lovers think and feel, into the future,
For all those things that refresh a love between both you
        and me.
Just to hear a voice, a command of
Basic communications, we have known for years and
        years.

To experience, is to know, and to know is to grow.
A means of enlightenment, associated with being.
Life for many of us and all of us has many roads.
Reality concludes both knowledge;
And experience shows constant change, as
Around the world it goes.

Queen of Arabian Nights

There are many reasons of the why
The "why" of what really makes a queen,
How she looks, how she acts, how she thinks, and then
    again,
She is ultimately a woman, a goddess, both good and
    mean.

A queen is excellent of wit,
Able to think and reason, solving puzzles,
A compassionate being to those all around her,
Realizing creation's meaning, overcoming problems and
    troubles.

She represents Mother Earth, loving and divine,
A god's head in feminine form.
There to give us life, there to give us birth,
For the love she feels is real; my love is mine.

Our bodies are like the heavenly bodies.
We move, we feel and orbit constantly.
Our bodies are like the marriage between
Adam and Eve, our first parents, ourselves in harmony.

Paradise lies beneath this desert.
It continues to keep us warm,
By giving us fuel across the world,
Through cold winters, rain, hail, and any snowstorm.

What happens in the past can
Truly affect us now.
A queen has grown in perfection.
Her spouse has loved her before, and he loves her now.

The Queen of Arabian Nights,
Rides gracefully upon her camel,
Quietly in the night, her shimmering skin shines and
    glows,
By the moonlight and the stars, by the sweet desert smell.

Her tiara gleamed upon her forehead,
Jades, rubies, and diamonds.
Her husband accompanies her also,
"With their child between them," she said.

The lady is most gifted and talented,
Skilled in charms and lures,
That keeps a mystical awareness
Of our scientific consciousness, God's, mine, and yours.

Should Satan try to part us,
No matter how far apart,
We are close in body, mind and spirit,
And closer still, to come, from the very start.

The Arabian Nights are most beautiful,
Because of the white and golden sands;
The white and golden sands of a dry and glassy sea,
Made by nature's creation, made by Allah's commands,
And because the miraculous paradise,
The most beautiful Garden of Eden, existed beneath Thee.

The Queen of the Arabian Nights
Sees the face of her creator,
In the stars and the glorious heavens above,
While she holds onto her spouse, with all her love,
With all her love, with all her might.

Life Has a Meaning

I. We were created by one greater
    Than ourselves, the Almighty.
    And He sees and knows all.
    We were conceived in love,
    To live and enjoy the fruits of this
    World shaped round like a ball.

II. Life has a meaning, a purpose, a plan;
    Life is made to be loved, enjoyed,
    And should be appreciated again, and again.
    Did you know that God was always watching,
    And keeping record of all that we say and do?
    He created us; He loves us, me and you.

III. Life has a meaning to be a blessing
     Of good deeds and to enjoy a family.
     We are both male, and others, female,
     To continue the right to life in eternity,
     Which of course means, love has no ending,
     For those who strive to live in harmony.

IV. Life has a meaning and a purpose.
    People should not just use one another,
    And should not be afraid to share love;
    For God, our creator has given unto us
    His unselfish and undivided love,
    Existing on this earth, we're loved from above.

Hope

What is hope and yet, but faith,
A form of wishing for the best
And a lot like hope; faith is true,
A blessing, a salvation like the rest.

As others have done before
Ventured on through life with hope,
For current needs can be great
We need the greater self, a greater scope.

Hope is more than just wishful thinking;
It is a determination to succeed.
HOPE is more than a fantasy.
It is the spirit alive that we all need.

Tell me about the greatest thing on earth,
People needing people, children needing parents,
And the miracle of new life,
The wonder, the joy, the marvel of birth.

What kind of life is there for me,
If not from a loved one, dear.
What kind of existence for any of us,
If there is only loneliness and no one near.

What does it really mean to live
If no one loves or cares?
People can become only objects,
When just being an existence, anywhere.

Values have changed when things
Become more important than *we.*
Materialism is there for the comfort,
But not to be more important than you and me.

And now, hope is the extra value.
It carries the love and caring code,
For it is a form of loving faith
That is sure to involve the quality love mode.

What value is a man who stands alone,
In selfishness, greed and spite?
Why a sad and mere existence,
Only to live with no one daily and nightly.

Life can be lonely and ugly,
When no one cares,
For hope is only for believers,
And the not so selfish, the prayerful, who dares.

Caring

To care means to love.
To care means concern.
A source of heartfelt intelligence,
A sense greater than to learn.

Learning begins with caring,
And wanting all the same.
They both go hand in hand,
For it's the togetherness of this earthly plane.

Learning is a form of caring,
A respect for things of beauty.
We learn through caring,
And the rewards are unanimously a duty.

Caring is foolproof and not without reward.
It has a certain golden rule,
A certain goodness, even the evil
Cannot contain, steal, or overrule.

Caring belongs to those who give;
The benefits are ever mighty.
Something greater than ourselves,
And evermore, we reap the goodness, daily and nightly.

Caring is a form of sharing,
OF love, understanding at best,
A certain type of people, unselfish,
NOT evil or wicked, neither making jest.

For couples are also composed,
Of personalities of men and women;
Some couples last longer than others,
Simply for this quality of caring among them.

And if there is a couple who doesn't care,
You'll know what really was about,
For these are the main ingredients,
To those who care the most, still together, without a doubt.

Keeping a Positive Attitude

What does it mean to keep the faith?
What does it mean to relay
A message of kindness and good cheer,
For we are all God's children each and every day.

Keeping the happy profile
And walking the extra mile,
Keeping a positive attitude
Means to let go of sadness, and to keep a happy smile.

Looking on the bright side and more,
Keeping a positive attitude,
Can mean a miracle just up ahead,
And inheriting much success and pleasure instead.

For good things come to those who wait
And as they say, love conquers all, not hate.
And to keep a positive attitude, you see
Can often change the plight of fate.

Ways of Love

The ways of love are both simple and mighty,
Little things, a glance, a smile, a kind thought
The ways of kindness and gentleness
All are very important to us and aught.

To be the things that make a day go well,
Things we learn as children,
From the wisdom of the elders,
The ways of God, of saints, and of angels, they tell.

Something good is happening to the young,
And the old all alike.
We never, ever outgrow the need
For love, kind words, pleasant thoughts,
With all our might.

A gentle touch can give life,
A smile can cure an ill;
And all my life from time to time,
A simple gesture of love is even an acquired skill.

Birds who chirp in harmony,
And flock across the sky,
Give a message in their travel,
Creatures of God keeping harmony alive.

The ways of love are a message,
Good vibrations and communications,
As old as life itself, positive thoughts,
Keeping life meaningful, never ending persuasions.

The ways of love are a feeling so dear,
To let us know, to help us show,
In all the little important ways,
That the goodness of God is ever so near.

The ways of love kept us young,
And happy for all renewing eternity,
A touch of happiness and innocence,
Lets us know there is still hope for you and me.

Having Eyes for You

Someone said with a smile,
"HE has eyes for you," and then,
Someone looked and saw the light;
Through our eyes, He sees both day and night.

Did you know HE sees through
OUR eyes, and feels through our feelings?
Because we are HIS creation,
All that we are, He knows all across the nation.

Every moving creature He made
Every man, woman, and child.
We grow in love and learning,
With blood, sweat and tears, the price is paid.

NOW we have money, a medium of exchange,
A little different meaning of value,
But, to an extent, we manage to arrange
A level of peace and harmony so strange.

When someone has eyes for you,
They glance with a glance of care;
You just adore the look
And don't mind at all for the stars.

When someone has eyes for you,
Hope that the kindness is also,
From someone from afar on high,
Because someone named God has eyes for you, eye to eye.

Here, we meet again having eyes,
And as the saying goes, we will meet again;
Love is in the air, and someone knows
That having loving eyes is how the living grows.

A Labor of Love

Tell me a story of love,
Of how people really learn
To feel a sense of right and wrong,
To know that giving is an act of
Love, and a beautiful song.

Tell me a story of love,
Like a little child's first love,
Knowing his mother's love is always there,
Because he knows she loves him and cares.

Why must life have its suffering,
And why some works go unrewarded?
But really no stone is ever unturned,
Because He sees and hears all
And records and rewards good deeds earned.

Life is a labor of love,
If you know what I mean.
You begin with a grade and later get paid,
For both are rewards to be seen.

In the Beginning

In the beginning, life was simple,
NO bills, no worries, lots of freedom.
Men were hefty and women beautiful,
Because they remembered Eve and Adam.

In the beginning, a man was a man,
And all those things that related.
A woman was a woman first,
Valued greatly with being a wife and a mother, not
    outgraded.

Those good personality traits too,
Courage and bravery and long suffering,
Are all highly valued still,
For our world has many accomplishments,
Of caring and loving, being human, of will.

NOW is still a good time to see
How men have achieved success,
And the women of their notes,
Are many, but the best are matched, with dates.

We were meant to be together,
The man called He, and me,
For we know a magic called togetherness,
And together they call us "we."

In the beginning, there was one half.
His name is called the man.
Then later came the other half, woman;
And together they made the world a happy home.

Like most families, the family of man
Has both its ups and its downs,
For in learning and growing, maturing,
Trying hard to be upright, not just clowns.

In the beginning, they learned about trust
And a variety of other emotions
Love, hate, jealousy, envy;
United we stand, divided we fall,
But love is all righteous and a must.

Believe in Me
(Song)

Believe in me, believe in me
Oh! if you love me, believe in me.
Some say they do, and others only pretend.
But if you really love me, at least believe in me.

Make me your lady, make me your friend.
If you mean more than that,
Then, why only pretend,
For if you really love me, believe in me when.

The flowers bloom in the spring
And birds rejoice and sing.
Do-be-do, do-be-do, to you I sing;
This is a message to you I bring.

Make me your lady, make me your friend.
If you mean more than that,
Then, why only pretend,
For if you really love me, believe in me when.

The flowers bloom in the spring,
And birds rejoice and sing.
Do-be-do, do-be-do, to you I sing.
This is a message to you I bring.

Believe in me, believe in me.
Oh! If you love, believe in me.
Some say they do, and others only pretend.
But if you really love me, at least believe in me.

Believe in me, believe in me.
Oh! If you really, really love me,
Then, baby, baby, baby,
Believe in me, believe in me.

Life Is a Bed of Roses

My life is a bed of roses,
Because my Lord has made it so.
Not like a slave or a beggar,
He loves me, my body, my mind, and my soul.

My life is a bed of roses.
My God has told me that I was His.
He feeds, clothes, and gives me shelter.
I am both loved and wed; this is the way that life is.

All that we ever have.
All that we ever are, at all,
We should all remember that
God made us, He created us, short and tall.

My life is a bed of roses.
Because my God is both old and young.
As a woman, He has shown me,
That there is indeed life eternal.

My life is indeed a bed of roses.
Because it is slow and stopping.
I have found eternal life, because,
My Lord loves me, so eternally, non-stopping.

Remember the Dream

Remember the dream, and let freedom sing.
Remember the marches that were made in Selma,
    Alabama.
Remember the causes of Dr. Martin Luther King,
And also remember to let freedom ring.

There were days of great misery and suffering.
There were freedom marches in Atlanta, Georgia.
There was much bloodshed and humiliation.
They sang, "We Shall Overcome," another song of
    America.

As members of the human family,
And for those who are neither extremely white nor black,
God has every move, every thought, every word and
    deed,
Properly recorded in the pages of time, past,
Present, and future to precede.

And for all those of us who know
The meaning of the familiar word *colored*,
This racial and cultural expression of endearment,
Was originally meant to include all of God's people of
    procurement.

Let freedom ring, so that we shall overcome
Poverty, ignorance, and hatred of all kinds
Short-sightedness, narrowmindedness, and envy.
Because a mind really is a terrible thing to waste indeed,
And should not be.

Lift every voice and sing
About jobs and careers, to improve the quality of living,
And lift every voice and sing,
That men, women, and children of every color
Forgive and be loving and giving.

Let not your spirit be tired.
But be you ever so uplifted and renewed,
To remember that God loves us and watches,
To see who really remembers the dream.

Lift every voice and sing about life.
Remember all the freedom marches,
With the brothers and the sisters, of all colors.
Life is not so hard and painful, nor as dreary as it may
    seem.

Remember what the Almighty has instructed,
To "Love You One Another, As I Have Loved You."
And with this in mind, love is still a good recipe
For peace and harmony and unity.

Be yet thankful for all the goodness around,
And constantly letting our MAKER know
That as being a part of this good earth,
We have yet survived and overcome death, birth, and
    rebirth.
Let freedom ring for all of the broken families,
And every single-parent family, household,
That the wayward and wondering fathers will come home
And seek their blessings of family living to uphold.

Let freedom ring for both parents,
And their sons, and their daughters,
That we can at last see and grow in society,
The goodness of God's blessing that we have
Truly overcome, and let God's will be done.

One Unity, One Race

There is here on earth but one race.
We are all called humanity.
And we are called both human and people.
Any other less defined characters are for us a disgrace.

We have many similarities,
Called physical differences and traits;
And also underneath the skin,
We have what is called varied personalities.

What does one look like, when mild and calm,
Or prominent and extraordinarily strong.
And how do we think? Is it alike and straightforward?
Or is it rather wayward, conniving and often wrong?

There is but one unity,
And there is people-wise, but one race.
Because we are of one family,
All and all, the family of God sharing heavenly space.

We are all inseparable, all a part of nature.
The sun, the moon, and the stars, we all share.
The elements of wind, fire, water and earth.
We are likewise formed, knowing the joys of life we bare.

And so it goes unrehearsed and unversed,
That the balances of good and evil
Are for each of us foolproof,
To know the good and to live it, is more blessing than
        curse.

Let the truth be known,
That we have a mission in life,
May we all be ever aware today,
To appreciate this life, that which is reaped is also sown.

And may those problems of the world be
For us to resolve and to solve not alone,
The Almighty is there to guide us.
Nothing is truly impossible, let the truth be known.

For there is but one unity, and but one race.
We, the people, have a reality to know.
That we share a part of the life cycle.
We are all connected in love, to learn and to grow.

Power

Exactly what is this thing called power?
Something good, something great, something gorgeous?
Is it love on the land and in the sea,
And even the universal heavens with Thee?
We know that it is something good and something great;
And that it works best through love than with hate.
Would you believe the envy and jealousy involved?
Even the children are power-conscious to date.
A ball of fire, loads of water and land,
Some call it earth from out of the universe,
And say it was not just a mistake,
Because somebody made us exist, and here we stand.

Now tell me something good, and tell it nice and new.
We hear, and we see, and we feel.
Now tell me something very exciting,
Exactly how did and who started all this; is it real?
Well, now let's all get back to power,
Which has many samplings of interesting examples,
Like the surprise of a fight for what's right,
And then, again, simply as joyously as the music we sing.
This thing that we call power,
Ministers and preachers can get so excited.
They describe to us how wonderful this thing is,
And how humongously great, and how mighty.

Let's talk with such joy and such glee,
About this wonderful thing called power,
Which is always usually colossal and big.
Power can also be the beauty and the charm,
From real hair, which is thought to be a wig.
The religious say it's something spiritual

And something we can never really own.
The righteous say it comes from and belongs to God,
Something truly supernatural, and universally unknown.
Well, let's talk a little more,
About this exciting something called power,
That comes along with the moon, the stars, and the sun.
Power is more than just an earthly thing, the breathing
    ones.

Life is great and beautiful,
And it can be ever so big, or ever so small.
Power has no set or measured dimension,
Simply shared for only a short while by all.
Power is shared by living,
A plane which, for us is only one-dimension,
Because we exist to enjoy it, as some do.
We how know, it is at least a wonderful descension.
Power has many planes and many meanings,
Some of which, we still yet do not understand.
But, at least we know this much;
It is shared somewhat, from a life-force called God,
Then on to man. . . .

Christmas Day

Today is Christmas Day,
The day that the Christ Child was born,
It marks the time in humanity,
That all of society must remember, we too are reborn.
This day marks a time of joy and celebration,
That remembers three wise kings,
From a faraway land called the Orient;
Bearing gifts of good fragrance and gold, so it went.
Christmas is a time of good cheer and giving,
A time for all to remember why we are living;
To be a part of this glorious worldly creation,
Enjoying life and working too, a likely realization.

Jesus was the Christ child, of wonder and glory, too.
He served as a model for all to follow.
He taught and instructed us of morals and parables,
And of the right way, to live for both me and for you.
Even today, the history repeats itself,
Of how even a miracle-maker, such as He,
Could come upon this earth,
To be loved and appreciated by some
And despised by others, for claiming to be God's Son.
Christmas is a time of rejoicing and happiness,
For people all over the world
To stop and realize what life is really all about,
A time to reflect and to check our hearts, no doubt.

Opening up our hearts and showing love,
Is one of the Christ child's first teachings,
To say that God truly loves us,
And that we do the same with each other, steadily
        reaching.

We should praise Him and really realize
Our dreams and hopes, He knows,
That deep down within our hearts,
He knows our thoughts and feelings, our souls.
Christmastide is a holiday of hope and good cheer,
When men remember the gift-giving,
The time of remembered hope and joy,
We recollect a time and a meaning for living.

Being true, being real, being good;
Being as sincere and as genuine as possible,
Maintaining a standard of reality, and more,
Accomplishing goals and dreams and good deeds galore.
Telling a story about Jesus Christ,
Is like telling a story about
The greatest man who ever lived,
A supreme and glorious being, who lived to give.
An unselfish and remarkable soul to behold;
A man of extraordinary personality and charm.
An ultimate reflection of Universal Love,
Deemed gloriously supreme, from the heavens above.

The Sea

Wide and deep is the ocean,
Full of variety and diversity to be,
Many fish of every size and color,
Full of life, full of beauty, the great sea.
Sea horses swim and curl in splendor.
Clams, oysters and mollusks, in hard shells,
Hold tight their precious food and gems,
Unlike the many-legged octopus, swimming so wide, so
    well.
Jelly fish are clear and colorful.
They can also sting to the touch.
Coiled and all glued together,
Gummy and sticky, in beautiful designs and such.

Seaweed and plankton, and other sea plants
Are food for the fish, as they wish,
Not only are they food, but they are also home,
For many schools of every sort of fish.
A world under water, a world all its own.
There is so much beautiful life.
Even earlier civilizations are buried there,
With many rich and mysterious stories to dare.
Many worlds have lived before us,
Full of knowledge and wisdom so true,
Including other lost worlds and continents,
Stepping stones that lead us to today,
Between the waters and the sky so blue.

A world under water, pleasant and alive,
There are caverns and hills and mountains,
Even pure and natural hot springs.
The sea hides secrets to keep and to sustain.
Underground caves, hidden communities,
Yet untouched by human civilization.
Lifestyles beyond our perception and realization,
Different as a code of ethics, within reason.
We are a part of nature, we are a part of the sea.
It has been said that all life evolved,
From out of the water,
And from its origin, we came to be.

All of the elements are still the same,
Fire, and water, and wind, and earth.
Of these four elements, we evolved.
We remain yet very much the same, resolved.
The sea holds life and secrets, many,
To keep and to maintain the earth.
The sea feeds and nurtures humanity.
There is plenty for all, there is plenty.
Water holds life, it replenishes.
Without it, we would all perish,
If only we could realize and remember
The beauty of life, the water, our existence, we should
    cherish.

Follow Your Nose

Following your nose is a saying,
To use your intuition, and using your senses,
A type of sensory language, more at body language,
Something we all have, more a reality than any pretenses.
Following your nose carries with it a tone,
A tone and knowledge of vibrations,
Felt from top to nose.
A kind of homing in on inclination in the bone.
Before we have ever learned to talk.
And even longer than that; before we walked,
The sensory smell was there on in,
A sense of feeling and knowing when.

Sometimes talk is just not enough,
As many people do not listen anyway.
Thoughts are expressed in many ways,
Language which is verbal, physical and sensory.
Top of the head vision is like a television
And is kind of an inner thought thing.
Sometimes the thoughts are only dreams.
And at other times these thoughts bloom forth from the
     scenes,
From the seams of our minds,
To the very depths of our toes,
Can really be felt with all kinds of ideas,
Out through to the very tips of our noses.

Being faced with a problem,
Or a puzzle of similar sorts,
Requires a system of rational judgment.
It requires important decisions even for sports.
Sharpening the senses is important.

Having a little ESP is good too.
Extrasensory Perception, I think is great.
Being smart and sharp is definitely the thing to do.
Has your nose ever itched?
And has it ever kind of wiggled and twitched?
You might also discovered yourself to be a little
bewitched.

There's nothing wrong with that.
You can either believe these things,
Or simply just leave them alone.
We might also discover connections with the unknown.
We all have a body, soul and mind,
Complete with all the required senses.
When a shiver goes up your spine,
Was it your mind, or a sense in kind?
What does it mean to just have that feeling,
Or to make a choice between these and those?
Sometimes knowledge and intellect,
Are just not enough, you must follow your nose.

Body Language, First Language

Before there was speech,
There was and still is, body language.
Before there was reading and writing,
There was life, love, emotion and body language.
In the beginning of early human development,
Even infants began the most gentle language.
Sight and sound, laughter and joy,
What hurts, what feels good, life's game to enjoy.
The very primary and basic values
Of this life have never really changed.
We are still the same kind and gentle people,
Created of mind, body and soul, amusingly arranged.

In all our differences and personalities,
Our different shades and actions,
Our differences, whatever they may be,
Never changes the science of touch so lovely.
Kissing is a language, a form of love,
Used interestingly by couples, boy and girl.
Kissing is an important type of communication,
A positive good and is pleasurable, all over the world.
Kissing is a good and proper greeting,
And is a universal sign,
A glad to meet you and glad to be with you meeting.
Kissing is a way of saying, I'm glad you're mine.

For many, a handshake is just good,
A greeting to be kept business, and it should;
But kissing is gentle touching, and yet
Just an innocent getting close to you, and don't forget
That we are in this life to enjoy
The being and the belonging in this life;

And there are many forms of communication to celebrate
And by occasionally just kissing, can be just great.
Eskimos do it, and so do we.
Just the warmth and the friendliness of it all,
It is really grand to be alive,
Whether life be serious or just having a ball.

Can't we all just be friends and get along,
Because we all share apart of God's domain.
Yet, man sometimes complicates it all.
And this has made living really a shame.
Straight from the heart, all honest and smart,
People should realize life's goodness, from the start,
To trust and to be trusted, to understand.
Life is a tempo to a musical note, high and low.
Life is a body language from start to finish.
And kissing is a positive note of love and acceptance,
A sure thing, a good thing, and a glorious sign that we
Should all love and know.

Return Lost Fathers

How many men were separated from home,
For reasons tricked or stolen from a neighbor?
How many men were deprived of their loved ones,
From departers, greedy to steal happiness and more?
Return, oh, long-lost father, return
And welcome loved ones long missed.
And be reunited with true loved ones
Forlorn in loneliness and worry, needing a kiss.
Remembered most are the missing fathers,
For they are the ones who are missed the most.
Mothers are often left alone to care for their own,
And worried abundantly at home and left alone.

Return, lost and wearied, suffering fathers,
Return to wives forgotten by others,
With children begotten in love and work,
With many sufferings created by others.
Return, forgotten fathers, to wives and children,
To be seen again after so long,
Seeing loneliness, heartbreak and abuses,
To be seen again, after society's cursing song.
Return to restore a family lost.
And renew an image that was forgotten,
Of how the evil eyes of jealousy did break
And the envious deceptive thoughts did take.

Return, lost fathers, only many and many more,
Of families, deprived so much of real happiness
And caught up in historical lies of centuries ago,
To be reunited with true love aglow.
Remembering men and women's suffering.
Some are seen, and some others are unrecorded still.

Of loneliness and much lost happiness,
From envied partakers, who plot and kill.
Return to the many who suffered so much,
And have been deprived by deceivers,
To be remembered by ones who loved and cared.
By ones who continued in steadfast hope and faith so
      beared.

Return of fathers, tricked away from home
And needing someone to remember, when
Life was so simple and easy to enjoy.
When a gift was really a gift, and a smile could win hearts.
We all have a final answer,
From One who watches all that breathes and moves,
And knows every single thought and secret
From those deceiving, how powerfully love still glows.
Return, oh, missing fathers, to homes,
Thought to be without care and attention.
All that seems to be missing does not have to be.
When the Greatest Father of all,
Watches over the land, the sky and the sea.

For Love and Life

Breath of morning and breath of life
Are touched by only true love.
For how and what is the essence of life,
If not for us being loved at all and of
A greater spirit than self,
One that sees all and guides His beloved
Throughout an existence so fair,
Throughout feelings and senses so rare.
Whatever is learning at all of caring,
Our mere being and existence on earth
Is intermingled and intertwined,
Since day one, our first awareness, since birth.

An infant's first realizations do not really change.
We still want to know, someone loves us, someone cares.
Even if we're sometimes selfish,
And especially when we're unselfish and share.
But a person's freedom of privacy is sacred,
A trust, a respect, a special pride,
To feel and to being real about our feelings,
How good one can ever possibly feel deep inside.
Realize in oneself, a greater self,
One that sends messages to the creator.
Believe, at least in oneself for truth,
Being trusting of oneself, to believe in your maker.

Always believing in something worthwhile,
Believe always in something true,
Never doubting in one's own capabilities.
Believe in the goodness of others, believe in you.
Life carries a monument of mysteries,
Some of which can be abundantly great.

Life can also be hard and cruel,
A constant struggle between love and hate.
Life is not far away from love and hate.
All are extremely important to survive.
Men seek for it always,
As infants, now grow-up, seeking care to stay alive.

Every child knows something of pain and hurt.
Every child learns the difference,
Between what feels good and what does not.
Those feelings are still inside, we never forgot.
Pain, pain, go away and leave me still
To be cured, of loneliness and sorrow.
To be loved and cared for by one,
Who loves me not just for today, but also for tomorrow.
Love and care we give to each other,
A great command from on high.
We learn to appreciate this life,
And to always remember true love is no lie.

Slapstick Behavior

Slapstick behavior is full of comedy,
Is good at some types of socializing.
However the tomfoolery will allow,
Silly-Willies and clowns love to jest and joke around.
Remember the older comics,
Closely related to constant laughing,
And guaranteed to keep you laughing,
Because of hilarious domestic comedy clapping.
Slapstick behavior is for buffoons,
Not really for serious-minded people.
But for the strange at heart,
More at the comedian's corner and children's cartoons.

Humor is sometimes good medicine.
It soothes and cures stressful hearts.
The ability to laugh is a blessing,
And is a special gift of life, ingenious and smart.
Too much clowning is not really allowed.
It can go too far away from reality.
Too much clowning can loosen the joy of laughing,
And can spoil and withdraw the happy meaning.
Slapstick behavior is good to relieve the tension,
Good to unwind the busy work day,
Good to enjoy our stay in the world of living,
And good to see the better side of us, to mention.

Humor for people is a happy comedy.
It helps to pass on and make the day.
There are, of course, things that are sometimes not funny.
But you would be surprised, somebody will laugh
        anyway.
Comedy is comedy and should be meant

To help ease the pains and stresses of life.
To relieve also life's many tensions,
Living is really meant for living, to be heaven-sent.
Some of us have reached that status,
With some few ups and downs.
As long as we try to do the right things
And remember, it sometimes pays to be clowns.

You would be surprised how much more and more
Some people actually make a living
And make career at clowning, for fun,
Which is really a kind of life-long forgiving.
Too much seriousness can sometimes be dangerous.
Too much tension is all just to mention,
Something to keep us awake and up all night,
Robbing us of important dreams and sleep, all right.
Not this lane for sensible people,
And not this route for good folks in town.
So joke a little and laugh a little.
Sometimes it is all right to enjoy life and be a clown.

Life

As precious as a simple blade of grass,
As pure as flowing natural spring water,
To realize all those things we didn't create,
The *author of life* must truly be great and grand.
As wonders never cease in nature's realm,
As sure nights are nights, and days are days,
There is yet much for all be thankful.
For knowing life is blessed still in all the wonderful ways.
So good are the buds of a tree.
So good are the wild animals roaming free.
So good are all the fishes in the seas.
Millions and billions are to include the birds and the bees.

An infant is born in one country.
An infant is born in another,
All sharing the goodness of our earth mother,
Spreading over our planet, still growing like no other.
Growing in likes and dislikes,
However many they may ever be,
Sharing looks and ways and actions,
Like fashionable fads, fashions and factions.
Even with individual differences,
And yet very much the same.
The discipline of continuance are more
And not just merely a constant game.

Life is more than just a duty,
Which is sometimes treated as a magical hat,
Whereby we simply just all fall out,
Into this realm called earth, to work and to play about.
Life is still a grand mystery to some
And just an ordinary routine to others

Learning to realize the value thereof,
Learning also to be good fathers and good mothers.
The logic of two's and coupling,
Is a *religion* of the natural order of things,
And constantly renewing all things, and the like.

However difficult this game seems to be,
This is a duty that we must follow upon.
This is the way it must always be,
To replenish, to renew both the land and the sea.
They say that all life originated in the sea,
Inclusive of the tiniest and simplest of life forms,
Each contributing to the life-ladder,
Inclusive of every chain and link, every wind and every
      storm.
Life grows more interesting, and more.
Every single day is a new learning adventure.
Life and being alive means existing supreme,
To experience many realities, joys and pleasures.

Human Qualities

The animal kingdom is infinitely rich,
As we are greatly included;
Beginning with a multiplicity of traits,
Each contributing additional qualities concluded.
Human qualities are similar and alike,
Separating the men from the women.
For only a short time, excepting love,
To communicate, and to procreate, initiated from above.
There are emotions of love, hate, jealousy and envy
Given to all of us for reasons, to learn
The differences between good and evil,
As a life-learning experience of great concern.

Qualities and gifts, and traits,
Help us to follow complexities sure,
To distinguish wrongs from rights,
Also a type of mind over matter, and more.
The forces within us are many,
To withstand life's many challenges,
Knowing when, where, and what,
Knowing how to accept changes in our cup.
Human qualities are extremely important.
We talk, we think, and we comprehend.
We sing languages of many messages on end.
We communicate also through machine made by men.

Machines made by men are good.
But, they are never more important than the minds
And hands that made them,
And never better than their purpose, a tool for men.
Things are things of amusement and work.
Things and objects are amazing,

When and only when people see each other,
To honor, at least, the creative nature ablazing.
Human qualities are uprising.
The ability to think has greatly improved.
We have come a long, long way,
By leaps and bounds, and strides of par-excellence,
    unmoved.

Excellence, in genius status and stature,
Is to dignify the meaning of being human.
Excellence in rationalization for sure,
Is to create, in us a realization, of sense mature.
What we have learned, as a people,
We have made life more livable and easy.
Making work less work, and more enjoyable,
We have achieved many new heights of knowledge.
And yet, our greatest achievements
Are still the same, of love and of caring.
Still striving for nurturing and maturing,
We are surpassing all others; we are still caring and
    loving.

Humanity

Man, in his obvious vision,
Sees others as he sees himself,
Sometimes in many good ways,
And yet, others not so good of self.
Man, in his distant past has
Come to realize the purpose of being,
Accomplishing many roads of travel,
And overcoming barriers and obstacles of seeing.
Man, in his vision and reasoning,
Tells us a story of ever-present existence,
Of being truly spectacular in thinking,
Of inventing many useful ideas in teaching.

Parables, myths, and stories all apply
To explain and show meaning to reality,
Learning about purification and healing of fire,
Learning about its source and power.
Humanity has its reasons and its seasons.
Man has a variety of shapes and tempers.
Humanity has its natural consistencies.
Man has withstood many obstacles, so true, so pure.
We are seen in many different cultures,
Just to name a few.
We are seen in many ages, colors and thoughts,
Given also many talents, unique in view.

Ancient people have left their mark.
And even now, many things remain the same.
Ancient people have left us great history.
And even now the story of life continues again.
Constantly, and consistently we believe
In something worthwhile just to survive.

Repeatedly again and again,
It is really good to be here on earth alive.
People's stories are people's experiences,
Lending and maintaining great sources
Of valuable experiences and teaching alike;
Useful in purposes, a rose, and a flower of nature's might.

Historical stories are usually of learned thought.
They tell many examples of failures and victories.
Historical stories are wealthy in nature,
Telling of people's accomplishments over the centuries.
Once there was a cave man,
Strong, well built, practical and crude.
Then came along other ages of people,
Witty, persistent, rugged, intelligent, renewed.
Once there were many, many races,
With ideas uniquely original and grand,
Leaving behind a trail of explicit mystery,
Giving another chapter in the existing and meaning of
    man.

Wisdom

Whatever is wisdom, if not all of these,
A proper perspective of values and goals.
'Tis true to believe in good and sure things.
We must strive to meet life's challenge rules.
Truth carries a continuous task.
Courage includes a lot of faithfulness.
And it is good over evil, it is truthfulness.
Wisdom is associated with wise people,
Most of whom are usually old.
Yet, even the youthful can be wise,
With plain and simple virtues of gold.

Plain and simple virtues are good,
Essential to the ways of life and living.
Sometimes conflicting with so-called norms;
Life's values never change, some taking and some giving.
Sometimes the young are rather honest.
They are yet, very much the same.
Life's needs are very much the same as ever.
Living and loving are often a survival game.
These needs never change, they never stop.
It is a wise man or woman, to be truthful,
To follow one's own intuition,
To live a wholesome and fulfilling mission.

Self-esteem is always very important.
Wise people should at least believe in self.
As self-respecting people should be,
And remember that God is the final judge, eternally.
Carry oneself as a role model.
Carry oneself as a model for others.
One never knows who is watching,

For most of us are either fathers or mothers (parents).
Regardless what the role, or mission,
Every human being is thought to be unique.
Most are mindful of self-honesty.
We will not live forever, a time clock to beat.

Whatever we set out to do, or how,
We must be ever willing, at least to do our best.
Striving for perfection and excellence,
Some achieve a task better than the rest.
People are ever so envious and critical.
They are usually judgmental and cruel,
Not knowing the path of each individual,
And, in so doing, violate the "Golden Rule."
How can one judge another,
And yet, not judge oneself, and more?
Our eyes are not the only eyes that see,
To see our own deeds, to truly have wisdom, indeed.

Love Has No Barriers
(Song)

With every beat of my heart,
I knew from the start,
That you were the one for me.
And with that
Love has no barriers, as you can plainly see.

REFRAIN:
Love has no barriers.
Oh! no, Oh! no, it's true.
My love for you has no barriers.
Love has no barriers, darling, it's true.

Since the day we first met,
Even now, I still have no regrets.
Of all the conflicts we've ever had,
There were times that I doubted you.
And I even thought that you were mad.

But even now, as time has gone by.
And others have tried to keep us apart,
My true feelings were my original feelings.
With you, I now know are still real,
Just as they were all the time, from the very start.

(REFRAIN AGAIN)
Now that we are back together,
Through rain, snow, sleet, hail and wind,
We are like birds of a feather,
That flock and join together,
All the way to eternity, with no end.
I've said it before, and I'll say it again . . .
(REFRAIN)

Never Let Go

(Song)

Music has a language all of its own.
Flowers have a natural beauty, authentically shown.
Birds and bees both travel between flowers and trees,
And we both have a love so strong
That still brings us to our knees.

What is this madness, this power so
Strong, so magnificent and pleasant?
It sends out a message so willing,
So thrilling, it says, never let go.

REFRAIN:
Never let go, never let go.
A feeling so good, like it always should.
This is how we know this love is so,
Real, so real, so real.
We never, ever want to let go.

And this is how the world of love
Stays alive and wonderfully afloat.
This ever so magical voyage in life,
Pleasure and joy, in living, on the high seas,
Of the love boat.

Tell me over and over again,
What you said before,
To keep me ever recharged,
With this power called love; it can't be a sin.

Because, you always monopolize my thoughts,
And keep coming back to my memories,
Of life's wonderful moments, and all I was ever taught
About life and love, in general, precious moments
Beautifully caught.

(BACK TO REFRAIN)

Mind's Eye

The mind's eye is a brilliance of sight
Much wider and deeper than our eyes.
We see in many, many ways during day and night.
And we are blessed that life has its good-byes
For, learning cannot truly be achieved
Without sincere loving and caring.
If it were not so, then why so much misery,
In this life for some, because of falling short on sharing?
The mind's eye can see with the sharpness of sight,
To see, and to think, and to know.
With eyes attached to many senses,
Original purposes have not changed for present or past
     tenses.

The mind's eye is also like a dream.
We see things before they arrive.
And sometimes this is called a gift,
To see far ahead, and avoid trouble by taking a duck and a
     dive.
The mind's eye can see a pretty picture,
Of things promised to be fulfilled,
So that hope of a brighter day will come,
Perhaps even in happiness for two, as one.
The mind's eyes has many dimensions.
We see the present, and now remember the past.
And we look also at the future ahead,
Hopefully to better ourselves, to live and to wed.

The mind's eye is a totality of sight,
Not only of all daylight, but also of night;
And virtuously so remembering hardships of bitterness,
Of all faculties, past, present, wrong or right.
Who knows what value is, if not right?
Some know not the value thereof.
When some of us soon forget that God loved us first,
And all becomes more important than love,
And who is to judge another on our planet earth
When the blind leads the blind;
One thinking that they know all the answers,
Out of darkness, leaving many others behind.

The mind's eye records history, all.
The least matter of importance is remembered,
By any stone unturned, any simple little happening,
A kind thought can make a short individual tall.
The mind's eye is the sight of glory.
It leads one where another follows.
A sight of glory is a victory won;
And in reality, a thought is a powerful story.
The mind's eye is peaceful and still.
It is really full of both loving care and of love.
Some so great, soon forget the little things,
When greatness always comes from another much greater,
     from above.

Love's Touch

Love's touch means so very much,
A spark of life, a miracle,
Because we believe from the start
That life means so much in unity's circle.
Life is a recycle; it goes through stages,
From conception to birth,
Then from infancy to adulthood.
We see, we grow, we develop with worth.
Love's touch, is the touch of joy.
We live and we rejuvenate from it.
Love's touch gives a spark of life,
From the heavens up above, to where we sit.

Whatever we say or do.
Whatever we know or learn.
Some things in this life never change,
And that we all need love, as a gift, to yearn.
Love's touch is yet greater than self.
It truly has a spiritual meaning,
For it is truly supreme and sublime.
It is also a gift of life, which flows like fine wine.
To stay alive, to stay healthy, to live,
We never outgrow the need for love.
Not ever, and yet, whatever we do,
Love's touch still and always comes from above.

Look into the eyes of an infant,
And what do you see?
Always a look of youthfulness and joy,
And of course, trustfulness, beauty for both girl and boy.
Love's touch has a unique meaning,
One that we all should forever know

That when we feel the warmth of love,
Both the body, the mind, and the spirit will grow.
There is no greater knowledge than this.
There is always a message,
In a warm and tender kiss.
There is no greater happiness over love and bliss.

Love's touch can rekindle life anew
And can keep it ever so precious.
Love can save a dying heart,
And can also restore life, so willing, so new.
Even for those who are not so young.
There is a continuous hope and need.
There is always a place for happiness.
And love's touch will cure a broken heart indeed.
Love's touch can be felt around the world,
And also in reality, as well as a dream.
We never, ever outgrow the need for love.
Love made us and should keep us, always to redeem.

Tokens of Love

Tokens of love, from above
We need down here on earth.
We suffer much and hunger much.
For those tokens of love from above.
Kind words are true to start the day.
Kind thoughts can tell a happy story.
But when people argue and fuss
Over not much, the day is ruined very much.
Tokens of love in soft and quiet prayer,
Is good to remember our Maker
Because it was He who showed us the way.
And with life, He is both giver and taker.

Trying to do good sometimes gets trampled,
In a life of many disappointments.
Others are not always caring.
Their roads are very different and overbearing.
Tokens of love can tell the truth.
A good heart never lies or fails,
For we truly need to be more caring.
Our very existence can be golden, or as hard as nails.
Tokens of love, for some, seem so scarce . . .
And such a hard and difficult task.
Simply to live in peace and to get along,
Is not really so much to ask.

There are many thoughts in our minds.
Many are good and some are not.
However we wish to read in thought.
Many of us remember the love, but others have forgot.
They have forgot because they hate.
And hate is surely not the way.

We nurture our lives with love and care,
And should always be ever so mindful every day.
A gift of thought, a gift of touch,
Or a gift of simply something nice to say
Can rekindle the reminders of love,
Even to uplift reality of why we're here anyway.

Not in hate, not in strife, not in misery,
Not in fear of each other,
And certainly not in getting along,
Because earth is our home and here is where we belong.
Why must it be miserable and intolerable?
And can we shut out the jealousy and hate?
Why must there be mistrust?
And why must there be tomorrow to debate?
Tokens of love can be wealthy, happy and wise.
They can show us a very rich and rewarding life,
Full of honors and awards and moments,
Yet to be happier still, endless tokens of love with
    compliments.

Tender Moments

Tender moments I do share,
Of everything I ever knew.
Breath of life, of toil and strife,
My every moment, I think of you.
When I see the light
That shines in your eyes,
My heart delights in heavenly thoughts;
And the joy we share dispels all lies.
Tender moments are precious still,
And then, as time goes on,
May paradise continue to survive.
And may our happiness continue on.

People like you are special, too.
You have somewhat lit up my life.
And then, again, I often have thought
Of once again saying, I do.
Tender moments wake us up,
Of our reality and true purpose,
To enjoy this life, while we live.
Not always in taking, but sometimes enjoying to give.
What does love mean in this life?
Is it a myth or a reality so true?
Bringing people down to earth,
Continuing on from the day of our birth, anew.

Tender moments are precious still.
And then as time goes on,
Sometimes loaded with sweat and hard work,
And maintaining a balance between right and wrong.
Tell a story so sad and so true,
Of people, who have forgotten to love,

The very basic needs of this life,
The unhappy, non-believers of strife.
Bring back the oldies, but goodies,
The old love songs, of not so long ago.
Bring back the good old days,
When glory and paradise survived any show.

Bring back all those things that
Gave us the very good feelings inside,
Feelings of belonging and happiness,
Those feelings of worth and pride.
Let not today be just another passing glory,
Of song, of dance, and fleeting moments.
Let not today go by so fast,
That we miss the true joy of life, simply to be content.
Tender moments, oh, tender moments, people will always
    be
Remembering the good things of life,
Remembering what makes life just worth living,
And how to love, and how to be so very, very happy.

For Goodness Sake

For all the good that God
Has dutifully and meticulously created,
Why in heaven's name have men distorted,
Changed things around, reversed and hated?
For all the things good that nature has made,
Why is so much of life made so miserable?
Of mere existence made so difficult,
So that in so many ways, we have paid.
More and more and more, there is less.
Less happiness of the normal kind,
Things that life came along with us,
Was once a part of our lives, now to remind.

Artificial exchanges of living we now have,
Exchanging simple pleasures, things we must now buy.
So simple life used to be and plain,
Matters here gifted to humankind, the same.
Life is basically good for all, and yet,
Why so hard and difficult still to get?
Further and further out of reach,
The very simple things in life, just to keep.
Say we now live in a better world,
All lies, lies, and artificially more lies.
Simply to trick the innocent, the saved.
And yet, God still watches over all our skies.

In spite of so many people in this world,
Yet loneliness and isolation become greater,
Because of the lack of understanding
Among ourselves, difficult to tell lovers from haters.
We still experience only a sample of paradise,
Sometimes in deed, sometimes in pleasure,

We still experience life's purity of living,
Some live simply to take, while others are constantly
     giving.
Why so much pain and human misery?
Why so many victims to so many lies?
We have lived lives of pain and torture,
Deprivation, socialization and deception for sure.

But for some who know and believe,
We can sometimes escape the great hate
That still exists as strong as ever.
And soon the masses will see the truth, sooner or later.
The silence of the innocence is still among us;
Families without fathers, wide open,
Exposed to evil, deceptive, wicked minds,
In the worst ways, open social mind traps, to get in.
However evil, however bad, and yet
The Supreme Observer is still there;
Wind, earth, fire and water are all around.
And yet, the goodness of deliverance is everywhere.

He Walks with Me
(Religious)

Today, I sat and thought about much,
About my own existence, my very being.
And then I thought some more,
That to reflect on life, a conscious seeing.
I know about a great Supreme Being
We call God, and He walks with me.
In many, many ways and forms,
He shows himself to us, from sea to sea.
Let me stop and say thank you, Jesus,
Just for being myself this day.
And let me stop and think again,
About all the good that came my way.

Sending out a message of life anew,
We learn something new every day.
However small, however great,
Just think and know, something good is coming this way.
I thought that many days have passed,
Some rather frightening and weary.
Many a day did pass me by,
That left me tired, sad and weary.
Where do we go from here?
Such a long trodden and lonely journey?
And how many more days do I need,
To know that, he loves me enough to walk with me?

One day I was born, new and fresh.
Upon this earth to breathe,
To grow and to learn about much,
A day in a new life, to know, to love, and such.
To learn, many many things,

All along the way,
To learn the differences between right and wrong,
To know whom to trust, and whom not, like a song.
Life can sometimes be so lonely.
And then it can be full of friends.
Children have parents, siblings and playmates.
And when grow up, the same turns on ends.

Life recycles itself, once a child ourselves.
Then, one day we are all grown up
To become the parents once were,
Just to know the other side of life, the day we wake up.
I know that life sometimes seems unfair.
Because, there are so many choices to make.
And yet, it can be so good for us,
Just to know that someone is there.
I know that my God is watching.
I know there is always unending forgiveness.
I know when things seem to go wrong.
There is a silver lining behind the cloud, because
He walks with me, like a beautiful song.

Our Family Tree
(Religious)

Bless, O Lord, our family tree,
And thank you for this day,
That we awaken for another day, to see
That we have come this far with our family.
The tree of life is wide and abundant
To grow and to develop so well.
To guard all the goodness, thereof,
And to continue this life cycle of love.
And may every new member
Know that we really care
To welcome aboard the goodness
Of our creation, our very best.

Bless, O Lord, our family tree,
For we have struggled and seen hard times,
That this life may show some pleasure and comfort,
For living is also, forgiving each other in trying times.
For all the dearly departed, we miss,
And to remember always in our prayers,
For they too have made their mark
And touch the tree of life, with their loving care.
And may we see our purpose in life fulfilled,
To try and to erase the sad moments away
However evil and wicked they were,
Let the Almighty take care of the transgressors.

There are no limits of sacred matrimony,
As long as we are true to ourselves,
And to value those vows, as best as we can.
And to respect our Savior, and avoiding sin.
There are some souls, that we may have done wrong.

They were innocent in these evil times.
May they ever be so watchful,
Though they never sleep, now speak, in some form,
     they're there.
In the absence of a true love,
May another try to recover much that was lost
However precious, the moments.
Even a broken heart can stand repair, regardless of the
     cost.

And yet, through it all,
Life should really be a joyous occasion,
With much goodness and happiness,
Like the first moments of discovery and caress.
Life continues and marches on,
Like the seriousness of soldiers at war.
Let the war be for peace and love.
And let us remember our true purpose, sent from above.
Bless this house and our family tree,
That no others should transgress those who enter.
That to keep sacred our reasons for living,
And to remember the One who saw us through it all, and
     be forgiving.